A 30-DAY DEVOTIONAL

7TH GRADE

GROWING YOUR FAITH

LARS ROOD

classes self-conscious decisive Performance Peer insecure Pressure adventurous confident ice sports mad fun band friendly fitting in nervous impulsive grades thoughtful anxious self-esteem cheerful electives

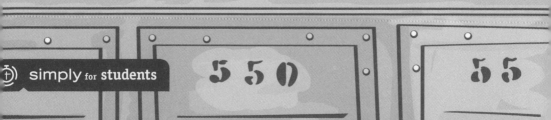

simply for students

550   55

YouthMinistry.com/TOGETHER

7th Grade
Growing Your Faith

© 2014 Lars Rood / 0000 0001 2378 3544

group.com
simplyyouthministry.com

Credits
Author: Lars Rood
Executive Developer: Jason Ostrander
Chief Creative Officer: Joani Schultz
Editor: Rob Cunningham
Cover Art and Production: Veronica Preston

ISBN: 978-1-4707-1823-7

10 9 8 7 6 5 4   20 19

Printed in the U.S.A.

TO SOREN:

I wrote this book when you were in seventh grade. Everything here was aimed at giving life to your faith and providing us with more things to talk about when we go out to breakfast on Tuesdays. I love who you are and who you are becoming. Seeing you interact with your friends, play drums in the worship band, grow in size and character, and just live your life is so incredible to watch as a dad. You inspire me to be a better friend, husband, dad, and follower of Jesus.

CONTENTS

SECTION 3:
MATURING IN BODY, SHAPING THE WHOLE YOU 47

FINAL THOUGHTS 71

A NOTE FOR YOUTH WORKERS AND PARENTS 72

INTRODUCTION

Hey there! My name is Lars, and I'm glad you're reading this book!

Seventh grade is a crazy year in junior high (or middle school, as I called it growing up). School gets harder, and you'll probably have to focus to stay on track with everything that's being thrown at you. School gets tougher, and this might be the first year you move from classroom to classroom all day. Figuring out where you're going to spend your time becomes harder because you get pulled in many directions. Sports, clubs, church, and family can get complicated. And friendships can get weird—people who've been your friends for a long time may not seem as close anymore.

During this year, you're figuring out who you are—and that's a good thing. Your faith might face new challenges, too, and you might find that you have more questions than you can handle—and maybe the answers that you were given earlier in life just don't make as much sense anymore. Figuring out how the Bible, faith, Jesus, God the Father, and the Holy Spirit fit into everyday life is significant as a seventh-grader.

Plus, this is really the beginning of the teenage years as you turn 13 (if you aren't 13 already)!

Despite all that, it really is a super cool season of life. You start getting more freedoms, and you have bigger responsibilities. Your choices and decisions feel like they really start to matter. Maybe your parents are trusting you more—and that feels awesome. This might be the first year you're in a church youth group and have a whole new experience that's way different from "children's ministry."

So here you go as you turn the pages and begin your seventh-grade year. I hope it's an incredible experience for you!

HOW THIS BOOK WORKS

This devotional includes 30 short things for you to think about. Each reading includes some sort of story related to seventh grade and some follow-up questions to consider. Most of the stories come from my own life and experiences (yes, I was a seventh-grader once— long, long, long ago!), so you'll get to know me a little bit. I hope that hearing about some of my struggles, wins, and experiences in seventh grade will help you. Maybe you can learn from my mistakes, or at least feel like someone actually understands what you're going through.

Each devotion includes a section called "God's Thought"—simple truths that come from the Bible and give you something to think about. Pulling out your Bible and reading it is a good, beneficial habit that will help you build a great foundation for your life. God cares deeply about you here in seventh grade—and that's a message you need to hear again and again and again.

You'll also find an action step for each devotion called "Activate"—a chance to discover something and live out some important truths. They'll take a little effort to accomplish, but I encourage you to do them because they'll help you grow. When we look for ways to connect Jesus to every part of our lives, then our faith becomes more real.

You can do these devotions by yourself, but you also can benefit from discussing them with a small group of friends, with a youth worker, or with your parents. This book might become 30 weeks of curriculum or simply provide 30 days of focus before the school year starts. It's my hope and prayer that these devotions will challenge you, encourage you, and help you prepare for the future.

And if you're doing these with another person or a group of people, I'm praying you have great conversations and opportunities to talk, ask questions, and kick around what it means to be a follower of Jesus.

SECTION 1

Owning Your Faith, Shaping Your Faith

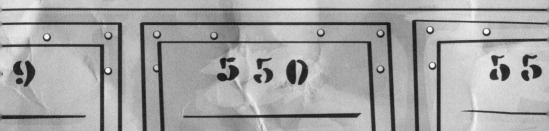

I grew up in a Lutheran church, and during seventh grade we started something called Confirmation. It was a two-year class (yeah, two years that felt like forever) where a pastor taught us each week about God the Father, Jesus, the Holy Spirit, the church, how faith worked in life, and a whole bunch of other stuff that I can't really remember. There were only about five of us in the class, and I didn't really have any friends there. Honestly, it wasn't the highlight of my week.

But seventh grade was also really good for me. I had been kind of a loner and didn't have a lot of friends. I grew up in a fairly remote place before it was as easy to connect with people as it is today. A church near my house had a youth group, and I got connected to it simply because that was where our Boy Scouts troop met. A couple of the guys in my troop told me about a weekly thing they did, and I started going—and pretty much from then on, I rarely missed youth group all the way through high school.

We all have the opportunity to "own our faith" in life—in other words, to grow a personal friendship with Jesus and not just be a Christian because our parents or friends are. For me this really started in seventh grade. I *chose* to go to youth group. I *chose* to read my Bible and to go on youth retreats. And what I got out of youth group was exactly what I needed. People spoke truth into my life and helped me discover who God had created me to be. I also had a ton of fun and made some really great friends and memories.

This section of the devotional is filled with specific ideas that will help you discover how to own your faith. I hope the stories, questions, truths, and live-it-out steps help you see how you can become even better friends with Jesus this year.

MAKING YOUR FAITH YOUR OWN

The thing I most remember about my church growing up was sitting next to my mom every Sunday and hearing her sing hymns. I didn't really like the songs—and there was no way you'd catch me as a seventh-grader opening my mouth and attempting to sing them. I just stood there each week and listened to my mom sing. Wanna know what's crazy? I know almost all those songs now—and when I hear them, they mean a lot to me because I think about how my parents took me to church and made faith a big deal when I was young.

Even though I didn't sing in that church, I did start connecting with songs that we sang over at my new youth group. That first year of youth group helped me connect with God through music. Sure, I know that not everyone has the same experience, and maybe you can't imagine ever singing in public. But something that year helped me care about my faith and start making it my own.

Think About

1. What adults in your life have an active faith in Jesus? How do you see them living out their faith?

2. If your parents are followers of Jesus, what are some ways they have helped your faith grow?

3. What moments in your life have helped you begin making your faith your own?

God Thought

Read Mark 1:16-20. I wonder what it was like for these young fishermen on the Sea of Galilee when Jesus told them to follow him. Why did these guys decide to follow Jesus? Why did *you* choose to follow him?

Activate

This idea is fairly simple—but also might seem scary. Find three adults and ask them a simple question: How did they become serious about following Jesus? If this sounds easy, ask adults that you don't know very well. And if this is really scary for you to do, come up with a plan to figure out which adults you can ask and how you might ask them. Maybe call them or send them a note somehow, instead of talking face-to-face.

HOW AND WHY TO READ THE BIBLE

I got a new "student Bible" in seventh grade. It had a section in the back where I could look up specific topics and then find places in the Bible that talked about those things. I found out later that it's called a concordance. That was a huge discovery for me: Suddenly, when I was feeling something, I could look in the Bible for a place that helped me understand it. So I'd look up words like *lonely*, *anxious*, *loved*, and *crush* and find things that would help me (though it didn't help me with how I felt about one particular girl in my class).

My student Bible was also helpful because it had extra stories that explained how to live out my faith. In fact, those stories were similar to what you're reading right here. They were written to help teenagers figure things out.

I wish I could tell you that since seventh grade, I've read the Bible every day of my life. Unfortunately, that hasn't been the case. Sometimes I remember that I haven't read it in a while— and it's usually at those moments that I realize I'm feeling far from God.

The Bible is such a great foundation for your faith. You might get stuck if you start reading from the beginning because there are some books that are just hard. But using the concordance to look up some key things you're thinking about and getting a student Bible that includes some stories of how it all plays out—those two steps can help your faith grow.

Think About

1. How much of the Bible have you read? Which part did you like the most, and why?

2. Which part of the Bible has been the hardest to understand, and who helped you find answers?

3. How much does the Bible connect to your life as a seventh-grader? Be honest and share any thoughts you have here.

4. What things get in the way of you reading your Bible? How do you need Jesus' help overcoming those obstacles?

God Thought

When I was younger, I got stuck thinking about how the Bible's 66 books—written over thousands of years—could really be a message from God to me. But 2 Timothy 3:10-17 really helped me understand this, specifically in verse 16 where it says, "All Scripture is God-breathed." Read this passage and think about the truth it contains.

Activate

Look in the back of your Bible and see if you have a concordance. If not, ask your parents or youth pastor to find you a Bible that has one. Then write down five things that you are feeling and see if you can find them in the concordance. Then look up a Scripture and see if it applies. In some cases it won't, but you might find that Jesus is speaking some truth to you through this action step.

NO. 3
WHY SPENDING TIME WITH JESUS IS IMPORTANT

I like mornings. I also hate mornings. Weird, huh? I like to wake up and start my day, but it's hard to leave my bed and get moving.

Back in seventh grade, I started taking showers each day before school. My mom would wake me up and I'd stumble to the shower. I'd try to keep my eyes closed as long as possible—even while I showered. Of course, at some point I had to open my eyes and decide what I was going to wear that day.

Unfortunately, some days the routine got messed up. My mom woke me up late—or I fell back asleep after she turned my light on. When that happened, my whole morning would seem chaotic, and my whole day would just feel "off."

Spending time with Jesus is an important part of a daily routine, too, because it helps you stay focused. How long that time needs to be or what you need to do during it—that's for you to figure out as you make your faith your own. I tried a whole bunch of different things, and at many different stages in my life I changed what I was doing. In seventh grade I simply tried to talk with Jesus each night before I fell asleep. This was great because it really helped my day end well, and the next morning would start with a good feeling. Later I tried (pretty unsuccessfully) to get up early in the morning and read my Bible. It just never really worked for me.

These days, I love to connect with Jesus by putting on my headphones in a coffee shop and writing. I also love being outside in nature—just hanging out and talking with Jesus while I look at the beauty he created.

Think About

1. What are some ways you spend time with Jesus? How has that gone for you?

2. If this idea is new to you, what are some things you might want to try?

3. How have you seen other people consistently connect with Jesus?

God Thought

Read Matthew 14:23, Mark 1:35, and Luke 6:12. Even Jesus needed to spend time with God the Father.

Activate

Looking for ideas on spending time with Jesus? Get up early. Stay up a little later. Take your Bible into the bathroom. And a whole bunch of other things. Try this: If you live in a place where this is safe to do, go for a walk. It doesn't have to be a long walk—just a focused time of walking and talking with Jesus. Before you go, think about and write out three things that you want to talk to him about. As you walk, pray and talk to Jesus. Ask those three questions, or just listen. When you get back, sit for a few minutes and think about how you and Jesus connected.

₦0.4
STAYING FOCUSED ON JESUS WHEN LIFE IS BUSY

Seventh grade was the first time that I remember life getting so busy. School, Boy Scouts, sports, friends, church, random stuff my parents wanted me to do—it all made me feel busy. Sometimes it was good because I enjoyed what was going on. Other times it was just lame.

During busy seasons, we need to focus and to make time for important stuff. Think about it this way: What would happen if you just forgot about your closest friends for a few months? Would you feel connected to them? Would your friendships stay strong? Probably not.

Did you realize that faith in Jesus is optional? Here's what I mean: You don't have a choice about going to school. On a sports team you get a set schedule of practices and games and have to be at them. Family events are often non-negotiable, too, and homework just has to be done. But faith—well, that one is easy to let slide if you aren't careful.

So how do you stay focused in your faith? It's different for everyone. I simply decided that I wouldn't miss youth group and church. I went almost every Wednesday and Sunday; it became my life pattern. You may not be able to do that, but you can "own" your faith in this area by figuring out what will help keep you focused.

Think About

1. What are some things you have to do each week that you don't really like to do? How do you get them done, even when you aren't highly motivated?

2. When is it toughest for you to stay focused on your friendship with Jesus?

3. How do you need Jesus to help you stay focused on your faith when life is just so busy?

God Thought

Read Luke 10:38-42—a story about two sisters, Martha and Mary. Martha complained that she was working hard while Mary just sat at Jesus' feet. What truths do you see in this passage?

Activate

It's tough to simply do nothing. Try this: Set a clock for five minutes and just sit still until the timer ends. How did it feel to take that pause? Write down three more times in the next three days when you can take five minutes to pause, do nothing, and just think about Jesus.

NO. 5
BEING OK WITH DOUBT

The youth group I attended was sometimes frustrating because it never really felt like a safe place to express my doubts. Because I grew up attending church, I had a good foundation about Scripture, how church worked, and what it meant to be a "good" Christian. But no one told me that I could ask questions and that it was OK if I didn't fully know how it all worked. So I sat in youth group and just listened to what my youth pastor said, even though many times I thought, "I don't get it" and "Why don't I just believe this stuff?"

I wish someone had told me it was OK if I didn't get it—or had asked me if I had any questions. But that didn't happen, so I became less and less vocal and open to talking about my faith because I didn't have it all figured out. Here's what I want you to hear: Be OK with being honest and sharing your questions and doubts. I hope and pray that in your church, home, or small group, someone has told you that it's OK to doubt.

Think About

1. Where do you feel safe telling people that you don't fully believe or understand something about your faith? If you don't have that kind of place, where do you *want* to feel safe expressing those thoughts or doubts?

2. What is one thing right now that you want to get off your chest and say you don't fully understand?

3. Who are a couple of people that you think you could go and talk with about your doubts?

God Thought

Check out John 20:24-29, which tells us about how one of Jesus' followers named Thomas didn't believe that Jesus had come back to life after his crucifixion. You can express your doubts because Jesus is clearly bigger than they are and will show you, like he showed Thomas, that he's real.

Activate

Having doubts is normal, natural, and OK. Write out three things that you struggle with, and then find a trusted adult to talk to about those things. Yeah, I know that can be tough and scary, especially if you think you will disappoint someone. But it's OK. We adults can handle it. We'd rather have you be like Thomas and question things than simply follow without fully figuring it out for yourself.

WHAT IF YOU CAN'T ANSWER A QUESTION ABOUT FAITH?

I hate taking tests. I don't like to get back an exam and see answers marked wrong. This fear comes from two things. First, my mom was a teacher, so I knew that high expectations were placed on me. Second, as a seventh-grader I didn't have a very good sense of who I was, so I always felt like something was wrong with *me* when I didn't get the answers right.

But I came up with a bad strategy to protect myself: I tried to stay away from situations where I had to give an answer. I avoided talking about tough things and isolated myself from people so they didn't realize I didn't have things figured out. As you might guess, this wasn't the best strategy if I still wanted to have friends. Having and being a friend means talking to people who eventually will discover that you don't have all the answers.

This can be scary if someone asks you a question about God and you don't have a solid answer. I remember one time trying to tell someone what it meant to be a follower of Jesus, and I fumbled so badly—I just knew that they were convinced I didn't know what I was talking about. But I have some good news: Jesus is OK when we don't know the answers to everything.

Think About

1. What's your typical response when you don't know an answer to a friend's question?

2. How have you handled discussions about your faith when you just didn't know what to say?

3. What would help you feel better prepared to answer questions about God, your faith, and what it means to be a follower of Jesus?

God Thought

I really like 1 Timothy 3:16. Read that verse and think about it. This verse tells me that in some cases, God will be a mystery and I can't know everything. I hope that gives you some freedom to be OK that you don't always know all the answers.

Activate

It's easy to find answers to many factual questions, thanks to online search engines. But answers about faith can be tougher to find. Take a couple of minutes and write three sentences expressing what you believe is true about your friendship with Jesus. Then look at those statements and write three questions that someone might ask about what you wrote. How would you

answer these questions?

WHERE DO YOU GO WHEN YOU NEED ANSWERS?

In seventh grade, Evan was my friend and one of the smartest people I knew. He was also really good at just figuring out how things worked. His dad worked at my church as the music director and at the middle school as an English teacher. So between the two of them, I could get answers to almost any question about God, school, life, or girls.

You live in a world where it is so easy to connect with people—and get answers from them. Just the other day, while I was on the other side of the country, my young daughter video-called me just to ask where she could find a pencil in our house. I answered, and then she said bye and hung up. Classic!

Where do you turn when you need answers? Do you have a parent or relative who is ready to help? What about a coach, teacher, or family friends? We all need people that we can turn to for answers.

Think About

1. Who do you turn to when you have big questions about life?

2. What things do you feel most comfortable asking about? What topics are uncomfortable to discuss?

3. What might help you to reach out to people more naturally and get your questions answered?

God Thought

Read 1 Kings 10:1-9, which tells about the Queen of Sheba and how she was impressed by Solomon's wisdom and the way he answered all her questions. As you read, think about how God can provide the answers to your questions.

Activate

I had Evan and Bill and a whole bunch of other people in my corner; now it's time to build your support team! Grab a sheet of paper and create two lists. In one column, make a list of things that you have questions about: faith, dating, parents, friends, kissing frogs, and anything else. In the next column, write the names of people that you would feel comfortable going to with your questions. Then draw lines between the two—creating a list of people you can turn to when you have specific questions. BTW, I still ask Evan questions about stuff—and he's still really smart!

HOW DOES YOUR FAITH IMPACT YOUR FRIENDSHIPS?

When I was in middle school my youth group attended dance parties a couple of times a year. Of course, "dancing" in seventh grade meant standing next to a wall and talking with my friends. I have fun memories of those nights and other times from youth group. We didn't have a big church, but almost all of my friends were from there. Faith and friendships seemed inseparable.

Your friendship situation may be totally different. Maybe most of your friends are from school, your neighborhood, or a sports team. Or maybe you feel like you don't have many friends. It's OK to be still figuring all this out. As you get older, you'll have more opportunities for your faith and friendships to interact because your friendship with Jesus will become more of who you are. I hope and pray that you have and will have friends who help point you to Jesus and don't draw you away.

BTW, I think I may have actually danced with a girl one of those times in seventh grade. But it was weird, and I quickly went back to the wall and my friends.

Think About

1. How does your faith impact your friendships right now?

2. Where did you meet your closest friends? Does the place a friendship started affect how you live out your faith? Why or why not?

3. What are the three most important things you look for in a friend?

God Thought

Read 1 Samuel 18:1-4 and think about what it means to be "one in spirit" and to "love someone as yourself." Why are those things important in a friendship?

Activate

"To have friends you must be a friend." I heard that over and over again growing up. So right now, go be a friend. Call, text, email, or use some other crazy way to reach out to a friend and tell them why they mean a lot to you. How did it feel to do that? What did that person say back to you?

FOLLOWING JESUS AND HAVING FUN

I'm super stoked that my two middle school-age sons have an amazing youth pastor, Nate. He's a really fun guy who helps teenagers experience the joy of following Jesus. I love knowing that he will impact my boys and their faith.

Nate and I met 20 years ago, when I was in college and working at a camp in California for the summer. He and some other people who worked at the camp had a faith in Jesus that seemed a lot more fun than mine was. As I watched them, I felt like God was telling me to learn from them. So I did—and over the next 10 years while I lived in California, Nate and I had a bunch of different experiences together that taught me about how to follow Jesus *and* live a really fun life.

Who in your life can help you discover the excitement of following Jesus *and* living a fun life? Maybe it's your youth pastor or a volunteer leader in your youth group. When I was in seventh grade, I learned a ton about Jesus from a volunteer in my group who led worship on his guitar. Whoever it is, find someone who can help you understand why following Jesus is the best decision ever.

Think About

1. Who in your life can help you learn about following Jesus more deeply, consistently, and joyfully?

2. What kinds of people do you look for when you want to see how to follow Jesus more authentically?

3. Is there anyone on TV, in music, in movies, or online that you believe teaches you some of what it means to be a follower of Jesus?

God Thought

Do you ever wonder what people who follow Jesus *really* look like? In Galatians 5, the Apostle Paul gives us a list of "fruit" that grows in the lives of people who are following Jesus. Read Galatians 5:16-26 for all the details.

Activate

Take a look at that list in Galatians 5 and think about which of those characteristics people see in you—or which you want Jesus to help you grow. Get a marker and write one of those characteristics on something that you can keep with you all day today. Think about it throughout the day, and pray that Jesus would help you.

NO. 10
BESIDES CHURCH, WHERE CAN YOUR FAITH GROW?

My faith grew in a boat.

Let me explain that a bit more.

When I was in seventh grade, we lived on an island and I had a boat. Once I was out on my boat during a storm. It probably wasn't more than just a slight wind, but at the time it felt pretty huge. As I left the dock, I wasn't sure that this was a particularly good idea—but I went anyway. Well, my faith really grew that day when I got carried away by the wind and wondered if that was going to be the end of me. I prayed out loud while I rowed, asking Jesus to help me get back to shore and keep me from capsizing. I didn't capsize, but I also didn't make it to the right shore—my dad had to pick me up on the other side of the bay.

My faith grew in other places, too. One spot was our local library, where I would read books all the time. I often tried to find a book that talked about people who had faith. And at that library I discovered the Narnia series of books by C.S. Lewis, which taught me a lot about God.

There are a ton of other places where your faith could grow. Maybe it'll happen at your home or at a relative's home or when you're hanging out with friends. It could happen on a sports team, at a movie theater, or just out in nature as you walk around and think about how amazing Jesus is. You just have to be looking for him.

Think About

1. Besides church or youth group or small group, where has your faith grown?

2. What makes that place significant for you? How have you grown there?

3. What are some other places that might help you think about Jesus?

God Thought

Read Matthew 2:1-6, which mentions that Jesus was born in Bethlehem. I wish you could go there and visit the place many people believe his birth happened. I've been there, and it's pretty incredible. The Church of the Nativity is amazingly beautiful, and you just feel like you are in the presence of God.

Activate

Search online for images of the Church of the Nativity in Bethlehem. Think about what it would be like to visit the spot where Jesus was born. How do those images make you feel? You probably won't go there anytime soon, so think about a spot near you where you could go and experience Jesus. Figure out a way to get there, take this book or some paper, and draw a picture that shows how you feel about Jesus' birth.

SECTION 2

Maturing in Mind, Shaping Your Thoughts

As I began to write this section, I stopped for a moment to pray for you. Why? I was feeling a deep sense of concern about how to best explain the importance of this part of the book. Here's what I mean.

When I think about my life in seventh grade, everything seemed simpler because we didn't have so many things competing for our attention or shaping our thinking. Imagine a world without the Internet or cable TV. What if video games weren't so common and it was much harder to access information? What would it be like if you didn't have a phone in your pocket and couldn't instantly communicate with your friends all the time?

I'm not saying the world is worse today than it was then. We had plenty of bad things and good things when I was in seventh grade—the same as today. I really love the world today and how technology lets you easily access things and connect with people. Even video games are so much cooler than when I was a teenager.

But it's important to know how culture influences you in powerful ways, so this section of the devotional examines some things that are good to expose yourself to, as well as some things that aren't so good. You'll look at moments from the Bible that can guide you, and you'll see some specific action ideas that can help you grow in a healthy way. And all of this is designed to grow your brain. Let's get to it.

NO. 11
HOW TO PROTECT YOUR BRAIN

In seventh grade, I went with my youth group to my very first concert, to see a band called Petra. Yeah, I realize you've probably never heard of Petra. Before the concert I had never heard of them either! I simply knew that my youth pastor said we all would learn something and have fun. I don't really remember anything about the show except for one song that they sang. The chorus included these lyrics: "Computer brains, put garbage in; computer brains, get garbage out."

The message was simple: The stuff you put into your brain matters. I've never forgotten that lyric because it's always been true in my life. When I was filling my brain with things that weren't good, I found myself responding in ways that I didn't like. And when I was putting good stuff in my brain, I usually felt like I was doing better in my faith. Fortunately, God is able to take the bad things and make them good.

Think About

1. What are some good things you've filled your brain with? How does that stuff affect the way you feel or think?

2. Explain what "Garbage in, garbage out" means to you. When have you found that to be true?

3. What are some ways you can protect your brain from things that are harmful, destructive, or otherwise not good?

God Thought

Isaiah 1:18 says God can make our sins "as white as snow." That's a good thing to think about because it means that God can take anything bad and free you from it. So even if you feel you've blown it and haven't done a good job of protecting your mind, you can be excited to know that God can make all things right.

Activate

We all need to learn how to filter things. It's the key to shaping our thoughts because it helps us clean out the junk and only allow the good stuff into our brains. How can you create a filter? Start by writing down a list of things that your brain needs more of. Your list might include words like *joy* and *love*—as well as other things that are good and helpful. Then create a list of things that you don't think are good or helpful—the junk you want to keep out of your mind. There you go—you just created a very simple filter. Focus on the good stuff.

WHAT IS WORTH LISTENING TO?

When I was in middle school, there was a strong movement in churches that told Christian kids to stop listening to certain radio stations and certain kinds of music because, well, certain people said that so much of it wasn't good. So one day I threw away all my "bad" music. (Back then, all we had were records and cassettes—this was before CDs and long before digital downloads!) I didn't really know why this music was "bad." Really, I was just throwing away things that other people told me weren't good—though it wasn't long before I got most of my music back again.

Fortunately, most youth pastors today have a much healthier way of helping teenagers filter music: Examine the lyrics and listen to the heart of the songs. Anytime I wonder if a specific song is good or helpful, I just look up the lyrics online. I also check how the music makes me respond. Years ago I was in the car with one of my really young kids. As I listened to a song with an angry beat and tone, I looked in the mirror and saw my 3-year-old holding up his fist to the music. Sure, it was a funny scene, but I was totally convicted because the song was causing me to feel angry. So I turned it off—and my son put down his fist.

You've probably had at least one argument with someone about your music choices. And maybe it's the truth when you say you don't listen to the words and they don't affect you—though maybe they are affecting you but you don't realize it. Here's my advice: Anytime you wonder if something is good for you or not, just ask someone. Ask a few people from different generations or stages of life. They will probably have different opinions, and it's worth hearing them.

Think About

1. What music do you like to listen to, and why?

2. If you've ever realized you were listening to something that wasn't good or helpful, how did you know?

3. What things help you know what's worth listening to?

4. How do you think the music you listen to affects your brain?

God Thought

Philippians 4:8-9 has a really good message about the stuff worth listening to. Go read that passage, which I love because it's not negative. It isn't telling you what *not* to listen to—it's just pointing out things *worth looking for.*

Activate

For this activity, involve someone else—ideally, an adult who might be able to introduce you to some music you've never heard. Ask this person to listen to some music with you and to help you examine it to see if it's good and beneficial for you. Have the other person pick some songs and then you can pick some songs. What good things do you both see in the music? Is there anything bad in the songs?

WHAT IS WORTH WATCHING?

When I was in seventh grade, I think we only had five channels on our television. (Seriously, I'm not exaggerating.) And there really wasn't a whole lot to watch on those channels. We didn't have DVRs or on-demand programs, and we couldn't watch TV on our smartphones or tablets—we didn't even have smartphones or tablets! So, Saturday morning was cartoons, Sunday night was movies, and shows for families were pretty much on from 7-9 p.m. on weekdays.

Your world is totally different. Because so much content is digital and streaming, you can watch whatever you want, whenever you want. But the big question is "What is worth watching?" Like our filter with music, some of this is easy and some of it is hard. Watching a super violent show or something that shows stuff reserved for the bedroom between a husband and wife—not really good for us.

But what about the gray areas? What if you're just watching a cartoon with "sort of" bad language, or you're watching something that you probably wouldn't choose if you were sitting next to your mom? The key is creating a brain/faith filter that will help you recognize what things are good and beneficial for you, and then focus on those things.

Think About

1. What movies and TV shows do you like to watch? Why?

2. How do you know if a movie or TV show is good for you or not?

3. What are two specific ideas or strategies that could help you filter the stuff you watch?

God Thought

Psalm 119:33-40 paints a picture of how God helps us focus on good stuff and turn away from bad stuff. Read this passage and think about things you want to keep watching because they are good and things you may need to stop watching.

Activate

Count the number of ways you can access media through your eyes. Go around your house and count every computer, television, tablet, phone, and any other device where you can watch content. It's probably a lot! Now pray about those devices and how you use them. Ask Jesus to help you make good choices. As you draw closer to him, those decisions will become easier to make.

NO.14
WHAT IS WORTH SAYING?

Has anyone ever told you that you don't have a very good filter about what you say? This has been a struggle my whole life because I often just say what's on my mind without thinking. It's a bad habit because I've hurt people's feelings and have even broken some friendships.

It's important to filter your words because you just can't say everything that's on your mind. You'd be talking nonstop, and no one else would get to say anything. A similar idea is true of the stuff you hear other people say. If you simply believe and listen to everything without any filter, you may have a tough time because of negative words, critical statements, and other discouraging things people might say.

My filter in seventh grade wasn't great. But I was lucky because my youth group helped me as I listened to the wisdom of my youth leaders and pastor when they talked about how to follow Jesus. You might already have an amazing filter with your words—or all the other things we've talked about in the past few devotions. I've been so impressed by some of the seventh-graders I've met because they seem to be really solid. But if you aren't quite there yet, ask adults or other teenagers how they filter their words, thoughts, and actions.

I do know this for sure: We need others to help us, and we can pray that Jesus will give each of us a great understanding in this area.

Think About

1. On a scale of 1-10, with 10 being "awesome," how good is your filter with the words you speak?

2. How good is your "listening and believing" filter for the words other people say to and about you?

3. Where do you want or need a better filter in your life?

God Thought

Read Job 31:1, which talks about making a "covenant" with your eyes. Read this verse and think about what it would mean for you and your filter—not just with your eyes or words, but in every area of your life.

Activate

You can learn a ton from other people by asking the right questions. Sometime this week, ask three people the "Think About" questions from above. What did you learn from them?

NO.15
YOUR CHOICES AFFECT YOUR LIFE

When I was in college, I worked with seventh-graders at a juvenile detention center—basically, a jail for young people. All of them had made choices that had impacted them negatively. I remember one particular student who looked like a typical seventh-grader, with the same hair, clothes, and language that you or your friends might have. But I watched him change over the next year. His choices put him in an environment where a lot of negative things began to grow in his life.

Of course, some teenagers at the very same juvenile detention center regretted their bad choices and decided to start making better ones. I witnessed several success stories of students whose lives were turned around.

You will make good choices in life, and you will make bad ones. All of them matter, and all of them will affect you in some way. The goal is to consider the consequences—good or bad—that a choice could have on your life. And when in doubt about what to do, ask someone and pray for God's wisdom and direction.

Think About

1. Think of a specific choice you made that produced a good consequence in your life. When you made that choice, did you think about the possible consequences, or did you just get "lucky" with the result?

2. How have your bad choices impacted you?

3. What are two things that could help you think through outcomes and consequences?

God Thought

Hebrews 13:7 says we need to "consider the outcome" of our leaders' choices. Read that verse and think about specific things you can learn from specific leaders.

Activate

Good choices are fun to think about. How can you keep track of them and make more of them? Write down five good choices you've made this week. How might your life be different if you added one good choice every week? What is one good choice you could make today, and what might the outcome be?

WHAT YOU THINK MATTERS

In seventh grade I didn't think many people liked me, and I was pretty sure that my parents had made a bad choice about where we lived. I spent too much time thinking about how my life would've been better if we hadn't moved to that island and if I could have stayed with my friends where we used to live.

Guess what? That thinking didn't do much to help me. I got caught up in focusing on what I thought should have happened, but I wasn't doing much to help change things in my life.

But then Jesus showed up, and I began to enjoy things at youth group, at school, and in my neighborhood. And then my thinking started changing. I began to think that I liked where I was living. I thought about how Jesus wanted me to be active in my church and my youth group. My outlook on everything began to change because my thinking had changed. It was a big life lesson when I realized that my thoughts and my attitudes affect me in all kinds of ways. It's true: What we think about really does matter.

Think About

1. Can you relate to my story from seventh grade? Why or why not?

2. List some positive and some negative examples of how the stuff you think about can affect your daily life.

3. When in your life have you decided to think differently about something? How did that change your outlook?

God Thought

The book of Proverbs gives us lots of good wisdom about our thoughts. Read Proverbs 14 and circle all the verses talking about ways that your thinking affects your life.

Activate

I often take the thoughts in my head and put them on paper so I can reread them and see if they make sense. Today, journal about some things you've been thinking about this week. But you don't have to use paper. If you feel more comfortable creating a video journal, go for it. Simply spend about 10 minutes writing or talking about the stuff you're currently wrestling with in your head. And if you're willing to take a risk, ask someone to read or watch your journal.

FOLLOWING JESUS AT SCHOOL

Seventh grade can be a tough year as you discover who you are, and one area that's sometimes hard to figure out is how to follow Jesus when you're at school. You may be surrounded by lots of Christians at your school, or you may feel isolated from anyone else who follows Jesus.

Here in seventh grade, you will have to make a lot of choices that can be tough. How do you choose your friends? What do you do when someone is being picked on? How do you respond if you're feeling down or unsure about yourself?

And then there's this big choice: How can you keep Jesus at the center of everything at school? I don't recommend carrying a huge Bible around and putting it next to you on the lunchroom table. You don't even have to pray before you eat (although it isn't a bad thing to do). What's important is to talk to Jesus throughout your day.

That's what I did in seventh grade. I would ask Jesus what mattered to him most or how he wanted me to represent him while I was at school. It goes back to the Fruit of the Spirit from Galatians 5—focus on those things, and ask Jesus to lead you on the right path.

Think About

1. When is it tough to live like a follower of Jesus while at school? When is it pretty easy?

2. What might it look like to put Jesus at the center of your time at school? What changes or choices might you need to make?

3. Who else at your school is also a follower of Jesus? How can you help each other in following Jesus?

God Thought

John 2:13-16 tells about a time Jesus got angry because of what was happening at the Temple, where people gathered to worship God. Read those verses. BTW, I'm NOT recommending that you act this way in your school, but you CAN think about how Jesus would show love to people at your school.

Activate

This idea is both simple and hard. Think about people at school who feel unloved or are treated like outcasts. Do something meaningful this week: Grab one or two of your friends at lunch and go and sit with someone who fits that description, and get to know him or her. Ask questions and simply be a friend like Jesus would be, and love them.

NO.18
FINDING A GOOD ROLE MODEL

Earlier I told you about my friend Evan—the smart guy who could answer a lot of my questions. Well, Evan was also a role model for me. Although he was only one year older, I looked up to him because he lived a life that I always thought was great. Evan was active at youth group and could play the guitar. I wanted to learn how to play, too. He was confident and seemed to really know who he was. I wanted that for myself, too. He was my friend, and that made me feel valued.

We all have different types of role models, and they might not all be followers of Jesus. If you love baseball, you probably have some favorite players. If you're a musician, you have favorite singers or bands. We can learn a lot of things from different people.

In our faith journey we need role models, too—our faith can grow as we watch certain people or get to know them. I learned a ton about Jesus from Evan because he lived what he believed. You may have some role models in your life already who are guiding you closer to Jesus—and if not, that's OK, because we will help you find them.

Think About

1. Identify three role models in your life, or three people you respect and admire. What draws you to them?

2. In your friendship with Jesus, do you have any role models? If so, why are they your role models? If not, why not?

3. What are some ways you could find more people to learn from in your faith journey?

God Thought

Read Ruth 1:6-18. I love the story of Ruth. You'll see that even after her husband died, Ruth wanted to stay with her mother-in-law, Naomi. Ruth loved her and admired her. Naomi was definitely a role model for Ruth.

Activate

It would be weird to randomly go to someone and ask him or her to be your role model. So simply list people you could learn from. Write the names of three people who could help you learn more about following Jesus, and identify specific ways they might help you. Once you have your list, go one step further. What if you picked one of those people and went and told them about your list? Take a bold step and make it happen.

GETTING UNSTUCK FROM BAD HABITS

In seventh grade, I got stuck in the habit of making fun of other people—not the wisest choice for a guy who didn't have a lot of friends but desperately wanted more. Making fun of people and also being sarcastic didn't exactly win me any new friendships.

At other times in my life I've been stuck in even worse habits that caused some damage to me and to the people around me. I wish it was impossible for us to get stuck in unhealthy things, but I am so glad that we can be rescued from these habits. Even this year, I've found freedom from some bad habits in my life. Jesus offers us a way out—and those things don't have to define us.

Back to me in seventh grade: It took a while, but eventually I realized that I didn't want to be the guy who made fun of people and was known for being sarcastic. At my youth group, as people began to speak truth into my life, I realized who I was and how I didn't need to put people down to feel better about myself.

You may feel you're in such a bad place right now that Jesus couldn't love you anymore. I want you to know that's totally a lie. Jesus loves you despite any bad choices you've made, and he is always willing to welcome you with open arms.

Think About

1. How do you feel when you're stuck in bad habits?

2. What bad choices or habits have you walked away from? What is it like to have freedom in those areas?

3. Do you feel like you're "stuck" in something right now? You don't have to write down what it is, but just acknowledging you feel stuck is a good step to starting the process of experiencing freedom in Jesus.

God Thought

Read Luke 15:11-32. Jesus told this parable about how a son made bad choices but was welcomed back by his father. Similarly, God welcomes us back if we make bad choices but want to be forgiven.

Activate

I falsely believed for much of my life that I had to face my struggles alone. I just kept everything inside and failed in the same way over and over again. Today's suggestion is really hard but helpful: Find someone you trust and tell that person about your biggest struggle. Share as little or as much as you want, but I promise you'll find some peace and freedom when you share.

AVOIDING DISTRACTIONS
AND STAYING FOCUSED

Back to Evan again. At one point in my life, I wanted to be a runner. Evan and I came up with a plan one night to get up early every morning so we could run on the beach. On the first day, he knocked on my window. I quickly got up and went outside, and we had a good run.

That was the first and last day I ever ran with Evan.

The next morning he knocked on my window, but I didn't answer. He kept knocking because he knew I was there. But I didn't get up—and my running career was over.

We can run into similar challenges in our faith journey, too. I've mentioned that going to youth group made a big difference in my life. But there was a time later as a teenager that I found myself so busy I couldn't go some weeks. And occasionally it would be a few weeks back-to-back, and I'd find myself wondering if it was really valuable and if I really needed to go that night. And I've had arguments with people and said unkind words immediately after times of prayer or reading my Bible.

None of this means I had walked away from Jesus. It just means that I had ups and downs, just like every follower of Christ does. Staying focused in your faith means remembering what matters most. It isn't about checking items off a list. It's about knowing, loving, and following Jesus, and keeping him at the center of your life.

Think About

1. When have you tried to do something but found yourself quickly losing focus? What can you learn from that experience?

2. Do you find it easy or hard to stay focused on Jesus during a typical week? Why?

3. What are two things you could do that might help you to stay focused on Jesus this week?

God Thought

Matthew 6:33 gives us some great wisdom about staying focused and pursuing the right priorities. Read that verse and think about how its wisdom might help you.

Activate

Create a list of what's important to you. First, make a list of the things you do. Then go back in and put them in order, from the most important to the least important. Don't try to figure out where Jesus fits on your list because he doesn't. He's not *on* the list—he is *in* all those things. So after each thing on your list simply write "with Jesus." Now go back and read your list and think about how you can let Jesus be a part of all those activities, tasks, and responsibilities.

SECTION 3

Maturing in Body, Shaping The Whole You

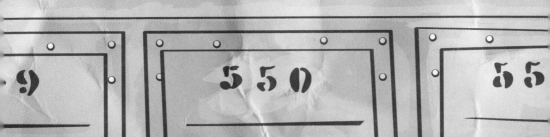

Seventh grade is probably the year you'll need to start wearing deodorant. Seriously.

It's just a fact of life that this is the year you'll start to stink (if it hasn't happened already). I've worked in youth ministry for a long time, so I promise you that I really do know what I'm talking about. A vanload of seventh-graders is a tough thing to stomach. And no, I'm not just talking about guys. Girls need deodorant, too.

But there's more to your growth and maturity this year than just your personal hygiene. You're likely going to get bigger and taller, and you'll begin to fill out and in—in other words, you may start looking more like an adult. Did you know that just over 100 years ago, 13-year-olds were actually viewed and treated as adults? Back then you could work a significant day alongside older adults, so you were treated just like them.

The "whole you" is more than just what goes on in your faith and in your brain. It also involves your body. The first time I held hands with a girl was in seventh grade. I still remember it as being so weird, and it really only lasted for about an hour during free time at a youth camp. Seventh grade also was when I started really figuring out the types of things I could do well. I tried out for the football team—I was skinny and not very good, but I learned a lot from going to practice and taking those hits. And along the way I realized that I was a much better tennis player than football player!

In this section, we'll talk about how you are growing and maturing, and what that means for your faith. But beyond that, we'll take a look at how all of the parts of you fit together. You are your faith, you are your mind, and you are your body. This section will help you to see the whole you.

BTW, an important truth to remember: We all develop at a unique pace, so you may seem way "ahead" of everyone else in your classes, or you may feel like you're "behind" everyone else. It doesn't matter—you're still going through lots of the changes we'll talk about! I promise!

TEENAGE BODIES ARE WEIRD

Go look in the mirror. You're getting taller. You may be dealing with acne. And you're going through all kinds of other physical changes, including hair showing up in weird places. It even seems like some guys can grow a full beard in seventh grade, which is both awesome and scary. But all of this is really cool because it means you're truly growing up.

A couple of years ago I had a cool "dad experience." I took my two boys to In-n-Out Burger, a restaurant chain based in Southern California. It was the first time both boys had ordered the Double-Double—a burger with two meat patties and two cheese slices. It's an iconic grown-up burger, and watching them eat meant they were entering into manhood. OK, that might sound weird, but I was proud that my boys were growing up.

I don't know what it's like for you right now. Maybe you feel completely uncomfortable with all the changes. Or maybe you're excited because you can do a trick you'd been trying for a long time, or you can reach something off of a shelf you couldn't before.

It's weird and cool—and God is in it all as you grow.

Think About

1. If you could ask God one question about the way he created you, what would you ask—and why?

2. What are some things you can do now that you couldn't do last year or three years ago? What's it like to see those kinds of changes?

3. As you're growing up, when do you feel like you don't fully understand who you are or what you are supposed to do? How do you handle those feelings?

God Thought

Read 1 Samuel 17:34-37, which tells about how David clearly understood who he was and how God was involved in his life. A few verses later, David fought the giant Goliath and killed him with just a sling, a few stones, and some wisdom. Think about the body God has given you and the skills you are developing. How can you use them for God?

Activate

God has given most of us the ability to run, even if we don't love to do it. If you're able, go outside right now and run really fast for about a minute. If you aren't able to run, then pick something that is physically difficult for you to do, and do it for one minute. How did that make you feel?

BEING A TEENAGER CAN BE CRAZY

My parents began to give me new freedoms and trust me more when I was in seventh grade. I'm not sure I repaid them very well—I became less willing to tell them about my day at school or to discuss what I was feeling. I sometimes felt confused about what I was supposed to do.

Now that I have a seventh-grader of my own, I don't use the word *confused*. I just say that sometimes he is crazy! He doesn't like that much, but I think it's kind of true.

With so much change going on with your body and how you interact with everything around you, you may just sort of freak out at times and not know what to do. But Jesus is walking with you, and that's a huge help to navigate all of this. His presence is like a lifeboat when you struggle to figure out what it means to be a teenager.

And just to be really clear: You don't have to have it all figured out, so don't worry. Following Jesus is a journey, an adventure. You can take amazing steps each day—such as doing this devotional—to help you draw closer to him.

Think About

1. What do you think adults don't understand about being a teenager?

2. How well are you doing with your responsibilities at this stage in your life?

3. What are two things you're super excited about in your current stage of life? What are two things about it that you really don't like at all?

God Thought

Read Ecclesiastes 11:8-10. You'll find some good truths here about being happy or "stoked" (my word) when you are young. It's a fun season, but it also comes with difficulties.

Activate

Find someone old. (I'll let you decide what "old" actually means.) It could be a relative, friend, neighbor, teacher, or coach. Ask that person the three "Think About" questions and see how their answers compare to yours. BTW, you may have to translate some of the language because "old people" don't always know what "stoked" means.

HOW TO TALK WITH YOUR PARENTS

I just checked my older son's phone and saw that he's sent about 1,500 text messages this month—and it's only about halfway through the month. Then I checked my own and realized I'm not far behind him!

If I'd had text messaging back in seventh grade, I probably would've done a better job of communicating with my parents. It would've been easier just to have little short conversations with them instead of the big question at dinner every night that I never knew how to answer: "How was your day?" I wanted to say things like "I'm struggling to understand who I am" or "I really don't get what it means to follow Jesus when I'm sitting at lunch." I wanted to share from my heart and be real, but instead I did what I'm guessing you may do: I usually just said, "Fine."

If you have great conversations with your parents regularly, continue doing that! Keep the pathway of communication open because your parents love hearing about your life. But if you can't relate to this, know that this still applies to all of us because on some level we are all trying to figure out how to speak to adults. (BTW, I use the word *parents* even though I realize you may have just one parent, or you have stepparents, or you live with your grandparents or some other guardians.)

Think About

1. When do you feel comfortable telling your parents what's really going on in your life? When do you feel uncomfortable doing that?

2. What things keep you from talking about that stuff with your parents?

3. What is one thing you wish your parents knew about you that they don't, and why?

God Thought

Read Luke 2:41-52. Jesus' parents didn't fully understand him or what he was doing. Think though this Scripture and imagine their conversation on the way home.

Activate

Think about the last "Think About" question and how you can best share your answer with your parents. You might do it via a note, a card, or a letter, or it could be via a text or several texts. You could do it one-on-one, or surprise them with it at the dinner table. Push yourself and do it.

NO. 24
WHAT IF NO ONE UNDERSTANDS YOU?

I was the poster child for the misunderstood seventh-grader. I played the clarinet in band. I read books in my room all afternoon. And I never felt like people figured out anything about me at school. I found acceptance and friendship in my youth group. But in general, I felt like I was alone.

Guess what? After 20 years of working in youth ministry, I've come to a conclusion that can help you: *No one in seventh grade thinks anyone really understands them.* This has been true for the thousands of students I've worked with over the years. You may doubt me because it seems like some people in your grade have it all figured out. They're secure about who they are, they have a lot of friends, and people want to be around them. But at their core, even they struggle sometimes.

So what do you do? Start by owning who you are. I did that when I decided to keep playing the clarinet. The next year I switched to the saxophone, and every year after that I was known as the band guy, and later in high school I won a bunch of awards for music. I also still love reading today, and (obviously) I like to write now, too. Another idea: Try a whole bunch of things so you really figure out who you are. I mentioned my attempt at football that didn't really turn out well. I was on the yearbook staff and even the school newspaper. I just kept trying stuff until the things I was doing finally lined up with the gifts God had given me.

Think About

1. Do you think people really understand you? Why or why not?

2. What are some things that you wish people knew about you?

3. What do you think is holding you back from letting more people see who you really are?

4. What's one thing you would try if you knew that you wouldn't fail?

God Thought

Read Job 12:13—a great verse in the middle of the incredible story of Job, who literally lost everything. But even while going through all that, Job still looked to God for help and strength.

Activate

Help people understand you by trying to fully understand them. Choose someone you believe you know well, and ask that person the four "Think About" questions. Then tell that person your answers. How did it feel to take a big step?

NO.25
HOW TO HANDLE LONELINESS

Loneliness often means we feel disconnected from people. But we also can experience that emotion when we feel like we don't belong or have any value that people see. If you've already hit your 13th birthday, it's possible you've started using social media. Several sites allow you to "like" things that people say. If you use one of those sites, doesn't it feel good when people click that button?

I've heard from some junior highers who sleep with cell phones next to them. They tell their parents that they use it as an alarm clock. But the *real reason* they sleep with their phone? They hope that someone will text them because it makes them feel less lonely.

Be prepared for moments of loneliness this year, especially at the beginning if you've transitioned schools and you don't know many people. That can be tough, and I pray it gets better. Sadly, even beyond school some of us feel lonely in our own homes. We sometimes feel that if we didn't exist, no one would care. Well, that's a lie and it doesn't come from God because he made you as a unique, amazing, incredible person.

You matter.

You have value.

You are loved.

Think About

1. When do you feel lonely? What do you think causes that loneliness?

2. When you are feeling lonely or disconnected, what helps you feel better?

3. If God has created you with a purpose (and he has), how do you feel about God when you are lonely?

God Thought

Psalm 25:16 says that when we are lonely, we can turn to God and ask him to fill us. Think about this truth the next time you feel that way.

Activate

We all need a "loneliness action plan." This may sound silly, but I used to save birthday cards. I put everything in a box that somehow fit the category of "someone caring about me." I still do this today with emails and notes I get. Go grab a box or make a file on your computer or phone, and fill it with things that will help you during times of loneliness.

NO. 26
BEING AWARE OF YOUR BODY'S NEEDS

Ever feel tired all the time? I remember discovering in middle school that I had the amazing gift of being able to sleep for long periods of time. For some reason, my parents didn't always appreciate the fact that I could sleep well past lunchtime on a Saturday! So they would get me up to do work around the house and get me moving. But there were also moments in seventh grade when I just had to "do" something, so I would get outside on my bike or go for a walk because I needed to be active.

As your body grows, you'll become more aware of its needs. But sometimes you may not listen and you'll just keep doing what you're doing and not take care of yourself well. I hope you don't crash too hard once you can't keep going. But you might.

God had a perfect design when he created the human body, and he created it to work in a specific way. We can't go without sleep for very long or do that very often. And at times we can "survive" on junk food, but then we have to change our habits and eat healthy stuff because we need nutrients.

This year as you gain more freedoms, do your best to make wise choices about your body and its needs—and ask others for help when you need to figure it out.

Think About

1. How much sleep do you get most nights? Is it too much or too little or just right?

2. How have your body's needs changed this year?

3. What benefits do you experience when you eat well and stay active?

4. How do you think God plays into this? Why would God care if you ate junk food all day?

God Thought

Psalm 63:1 is one of my favorite verses. It talks about how our bodies "long" for God. Read that whole psalm, and think about how your body and the ways you care for it can help you to have a deeper desire to know and love God.

Activate

Grab a pen and a note card and write down three things: (1) What did you eat today? (2) How long did you sleep last night? (3) How did you feel? Reread the card tomorrow and try to do different things in the first two areas—and then see how much it affects your answer to the third question.

NO. 27
SHAPING YOUR FUTURE

I've started talking to my own teenage son a lot more about his future lately. We've been trying to spend time together each week, and my goal is to just ask a lot of questions and see what he's thinking. I know that seventh-grade report cards aren't going to matter when you apply to college years from now, but you are starting to build a foundation that is incredibly important.

Remember that question you got asked as a kindergartener about what you wanted to do when you grew up? Do you spend much time these days thinking about that? Don't feel any unfair pressure—it's OK if you never think about it. But it is important to start examining some of the things you are doing and see if they line up with the future you think you might have.

And your relationship with Jesus is super important here because you don't have to just make decisions and then hope he blesses them. Instead, ask Jesus to be in your decisions and lead you along the best road in life.

Think About

1. As a kindergartener, how did you answer the question "What do you want to do when you grow up?"

2. As a seventh-grader, how might you answer that same question?

3. What clues has God given you about what you could do or be in the future?

4. What choices are you making now that will help build a solid foundation for later in life?

God Thought

This might be a challenging idea, but you can do it. Read the whole book of Jonah (it's just four chapters long). You'll see that Jonah didn't want to listen to God. Jonah rebelled, and it didn't turn out so well. But then even after he followed God's plan, everything wasn't perfect. Think about that.

Activate

Find a sheet of paper and draw images that represent several of the things that you can imagine yourself doing in your future. Spend some time praying over that paper and asking God to lead you to one of them—or to something totally different, if that's the road he wants you to travel.

NO. 28
SHAPING YOUR SUPPORT TEAM

We all need support because life can be hard. My pastor says something that I really like: "Becoming an adult means learning to deal with loss." That might sound a little depressing, but I don't take it that way. To me it just means that change happens in life, and how we respond to it is a big deal.

Some of us have really big support systems—family, extended relatives, and other people who do a great job of caring for us. Others of us rely on friends or other adults who have been there when we needed them. Sometimes, though, you may feel like you don't have the support you need—even if you're surrounded by people who love you.

I think seventh grade was the first time I ever said, "No one understands me." I'm sure it wasn't true, but that's how I felt, so it was my reality.

I've mentioned many times how important my youth group was to me. But it wasn't just the group that helped me—my weekly decision to attend and get involved made it a big deal. I committed to doing something that helped build my support team.

Commit to being a part of something where you can really be "known," because it will help you get support. This is a great year to grow in this area because you will constantly need it.

Think About

1. Where do you turn when you need support?

2. Think of a specific situation that came up where you needed a support structure—how did your support team help you?

3. Who are some people in your life you could invite to be on your support team?

God Thought

Acts 2:42-47 tells about some of the earliest followers of Jesus and how they supported and cared for each other. Read that Scripture, and think about how you could see this happening in your own life.

Activate

Building a support team takes work. So let's work at it. Who's on your team now, and why? What people can you add to it? Think about the people in your life, and pray that God will make it clear who you could talk to. Then, once it's clear, go and do it.

NO. 29
FIGURING OUT THE OTHER GENDER

As bodies mature, so do thoughts about the other half of the school—guys pay more attention to girls, and girls pay more attention to guys.

I remember this so well. In sixth grade I sat all day next to Michelle—my first crush. Then seventh grade arrived and I didn't have any classes with her. And on top of that, it felt like when I did see her, our friendship had changed.

I have two sisters, but the school thing felt totally different—I just didn't understand girls. And I'm pretty sure that you girls don't really understand guys. It's just funny sometimes how all that works out.

The Bible tells us how God created both male and female, and that there was purpose for both genders. So hold on to that, even if you don't fully know how to interact with them—God has a purpose even if you can't see it.

Here's some quick advice. Start by working to understand yourself. It's the whole "To have a friend, be a friend" idea here. Members of the other gender just like knowing that you have yourself figured out a little bit and aren't crazy. Because that's the reality, right? It's tough to have solid friendships with the other gender without this foundation.

Think About

1. As you mature and grow, how is your interaction with the opposite gender changing?

2. What things do you find yourself thinking about that might be new to you?

3. How do you think God wants you to interact with the opposite gender?

God Thought

Read Genesis 1:27-28, which tells us how God created man and woman, and everything God created was good. How can knowing this affect the way you interact with the opposite gender?

Activate

Find someone of the opposite gender that you feel safe talking with, and ask that person these questions: (1) What is something important about the opposite gender that will help me better talk to them? (2) What things should I avoid talking about because they are taboo or inappropriate? (3) How can I best build real and meaningful friendships with the opposite gender?

NO. 30
SHAPING YOUR CHURCH EXPERIENCE

Getting connected to other followers of Jesus means more than just attending youth group. As you know by now, I grew up in a small church, and my youth group was at a different church. So I wasn't fully connected to the youth group church. But my family attended our church's service each week, and that helped me get connected. I also joined the choir, which might not be your thing but worked for me.

I found that the more involved I got, the more the adults at church seemed interested in me and wanted to know what was going on in my life. They became part of my support team. The people who asked me about games seemed to care about all parts of me, and we all need that in our journey of following Jesus.

Think About

1. What's your connection to your church now? Is it more than just youth group?

2. What are some ways you've served at your church, and how did those opportunities impact you?

3. What are some ways you can get even more connected?

God Thought

Read Romans 12:4-8. Everyone who's a follower of Jesus has something to contribute to other people and something to receive from other people. Look through this passage and see how the Apostle Paul focuses on our attitude. God wants us to serve him and others, and he wants us to serve with a healthy, Jesus-focused attitude.

Activate

Do something well this week. Put in some extra effort on a homework assignment. Practice a little longer for your team. Do an extra chore or two at home without being asked. Whatever you decide to do, do it well and do it with an attitude that says, "I am honoring Jesus through this."

FINAL THOUGHTS

What a ride, right? Seventh grade is such an amazingly fun year, though after going through all 30 of these devotions you might feel a little overwhelmed! I hope that you've seen many truths from my stories, our questions, the Bible, and the ideas you can live out. It'll be so much fun to watch what happens in your life this year as you mature your focus and shape your faith.

I wrote this book right at the end of my older son's seventh-grade year. I've seen so much of this become real in his life. We haven't talked about all these issues, but now that it's all written, we're going to go through them together as I help him prepare for eighth grade.

Blessings on you and all that you will experience during seventh grade. I love knowing that this will help you grow!

A NOTE FOR YOUTH WORKERS AND PARENTS

This devotional can work well as curriculum for your youth group or small group, or as a tool to engage in conversations with your son or daughter. I recommend that you use each devotion as a stand-alone topic, giving you 30 themes for discussion.

If possible, read through the story, questions, and Scripture ahead of time. Consider preparing some of your own stories, either in place of or in addition to what I've written.

Read through the stories with your teenager(s), and then talk through the questions. Take time to open your Bibles (or your Bible apps) to read the Scripture passages together. And use the Activate content to give your teenager(s) an action step for the week—it will create great opportunities to follow up with a phone call, text, or face-to-face conversation to see how they're doing.

Ultimately, you know your teenager(s) better than I do, so trust your judgment on what to use, what to modify, and what to replace as you work through each devotion!